SUFFOLK in photographs

SUFFOLK
in photographs

text by John Burke
photographs by Anthony Kersting

B. T. BATSFORD LTD, LONDON

Title page The main
Street, Lavenham

First published 1976: © text John Burke, 1976: © photographs A.F. Kersting, 1976
Reprinted 1984

Printed in Great Britain by
Butler & Tanner Ltd, Frome, Somerset
for the publishers B. T. Batsford Ltd,
4 Fitzhardinge Street, London W1H 0AH

ISBN 0 7134 3111 3

Introduction

In the absence of television to 'put her image across', as the current phrase has it, Queen Elizabeth I made a practice of going about the countryside showing herself to her subjects and winning their allegiance. In 1578 she set out on a tour of which one observer said, 'I never did see her Majestie better received by two counties in one journey than Suffolke and Norfolke now: Suffolke of gentillmen, and Norfolke of the meaner sort.'

However amusing this distinction may be to South Folk chauvinists, it is rather misleading. The impression left upon a casual observer today would be of the northern county as one of sumptuous halls and large estates surrounded by vast, fertile farmlands, and of Suffolk with cosier echoes of well-to-do merchants and tradesmen who built compact little towns and villages rather than stately mansions. But such generalisations are equally misleading. Suffolk has had its bourgeois prosperity and its near-starvation; industrial decline and bitter struggles against the sea; but it has also had its kings and barons, and great nobles who attempted to link not merely their fortunes but their families with royalty, and lived to regret it – not, in some cases, living so very long.

What relics of earlier generations will the modern traveller still find recognisable?

Neolithic settlers dug flint from the sandy wastes now known as Breckland, straddling Suffolk and Norfolk, and from it fashioned tools and weapons. Even with the development of more sophisticated instruments of war and the chase there remained a need for this local craft: throughout later centuries the stone continued to be 'knapped' – that is, chipped and trimmed – to make gunflints. And decoratively it appears all across the county and some little way beyond its borders in ornamental flushwork, the blending of dressed flint with freestone into a black-and-white chequerwork on many a mighty church.

The Belgae who arrived in the first century B.C. tackled the heavy clay lands with their ploughs, and left traces of a few settlements. Two cemeteries of urn burials have been found at Boxford, and brooches and other ornaments showing strong Roman influence. The Iceni, a tribe which held out for some time against these newcomers and later, under Queen Boudicca, against the Romans, had many leaders rich enough to wear the gold or alloy necklets known as torcs. Five such were found in 1968 during building operations in Ipswich, and can be seen in the British Museum. Also in the British Museum, with replicas on display in Ipswich Museum, is the magnificent Mildenhall Treasure of silver bowls, dishes and goblets, which appear to have been hidden away in Roman times against the increasing menace of Anglo-Saxon marauders.

An enduring testimony to the threat offered by these assailants is the chain of forts along what the Romans called the Saxon Shore. In north-east Suffolk, large sections of the walls and circular bastions of Burgh Castle survive, though the wide estuary which they once guarded has shrunk into the innocuous River Waveney. When the Saxons finally established themselves they built a pagan cemetery outside the walls. Within, a large mound which survived until the early nineteenth century was clearly the last vestige of a castle built into the earlier bailey by the Normans.

Angles, Saxons, Danes and Normans have all added their visible contributions to the complex pattern. There were pagan leaders such as the wealthy Angle whose ship burial at Sutton Hoo, near Woodbridge, was accompanied by a treasure of weapons and household goods in gold and silver, iron and bronze, some of it richly inlaid; and converts such as Redwald of the Wuffinga dynasty, the first East Anglian king to embrace Christianity.

Another heroic leader is remembered to this day. Young King Edmund, defeated at Barnham in 870 and finally captured by the Danes, was offered his life if he would renounce Christianity. He refused, and legend has it that he was tied to an oak tree near Hoxne and used for target practice by Danish archers. After death his head was cut off and tossed into a bush. Discovering the corpse and seeking the head, his grief-stricken followers found it in the jaws of a protective wolf, who relinquished it and made off. Whatever the fantastic element in this, and whatever arguments there may be over Hoxne's claim to be the place of the martyrdom, the symbolism remains: a carved bench end at Hadleigh is only one of many representations of Edmund's head held by the wolf, and the emblem of a crown transfixed by arrows appears in many a church window, traced in stonework, embroidered into altar cloths and kneelers, and in the coat of arms of Bury St Edmunds.

The next invaders, the Normans, set up their own castles to discipline the defeated country. Powerful barons who had assisted the Conqueror were granted such gifts as Bungay and Framlingham, though the fortifications there are not the originals. Barons rebelled too often against their ruler, and then their castles were sequestrated, pulled down, perhaps rebuilt later, and all too often demolished again.

In this book Mr Kersting's far-ranging record of Suffolk has been put into a sequence which will enable the leisurely traveller to saunter from one part of the county to another without too much doubling back or going off at too many unrewarding tangents. Not that there *are* many unrewarding highways or by-ways in this spacious yet intimate region.

What we cannot avoid calling 'Constable country' begins along the Essex border, and as we move through scenes which the painter would still find familiar today, we meet the rich architecture of towns and villages which were once centres of a flourishing industry.

Lavenham, with its great Guildhall where the wool merchants thrashed out their problems and its massive church built largely from the profits on wool, is the most famous; but there were others of almost equal importance. At Hadleigh, a fourteenth-century poll tax return shows one man in five as being employed in the weaving trade. Kersey gave its name to a certain type of cloth. At Sudbury, the painter Gainsborough's father was at one time a clothier, and when the wool trade had finally drifted away to the West country, the town turned towards silk weaving and built that up during the nineteenth century.

Bury St Edmunds is the true heart of the county, redolent with memories of St Edmund, of Magna Carta, of Daniel Defoe, and of generations of craftsmen whose handiwork is to be seen on every corner, down every side street. And on across the farmlands there are other local joys: oak-framed cottages and colour-washed plaster; farmhouses with reedy moats, usually the legacy of clay-pits dug on site to provide building material; and everywhere fine flourishes of pargeting, the local specialty of ornate plasterwork coaxed while still wet into raised or indented patterns by means of a comb or trowel.

Last of all, the fascinating, treacherous coastline with crumbling cliffs and harbours sucked into the sea or unpredictably silting up. Those shifting contours have made the establishment of a Blackpool or Clacton here difficult. Lowestoft has a couple of piers and some amusement arcades, but has become the home of deep-frozen foods rather than sun-seeking holidaymakers. Southwold is quiet and still somehow Edwardian, making no concessions to those in search of fruit machines and funny hats – though, come to think of it, I have seen some fairly funny hats in the neighbourhood during the Aldeburgh Festival. And perhaps Aldeburgh itself is not so very different from what it was in 1819: 'The constant resort of rank and fortune, of opulence and respectability . . . the society of Aldeborough is gay without profligacy, and pleasurable without mingling in debauchery.'

Let us hope that Suffolk will not be profligate with its resources and will not debauch its incomparable beauties. Let the pictures within these covers remain true to life for many decades and not become merely historical records of scenes corrupted and destroyed. I like to think that folk here are too stubborn to allow their way of life to be overrun by invaders from cities and government offices. Truly it has been said:

'If you want to find a fool in Suffolk, you'll have to bring him with you.'

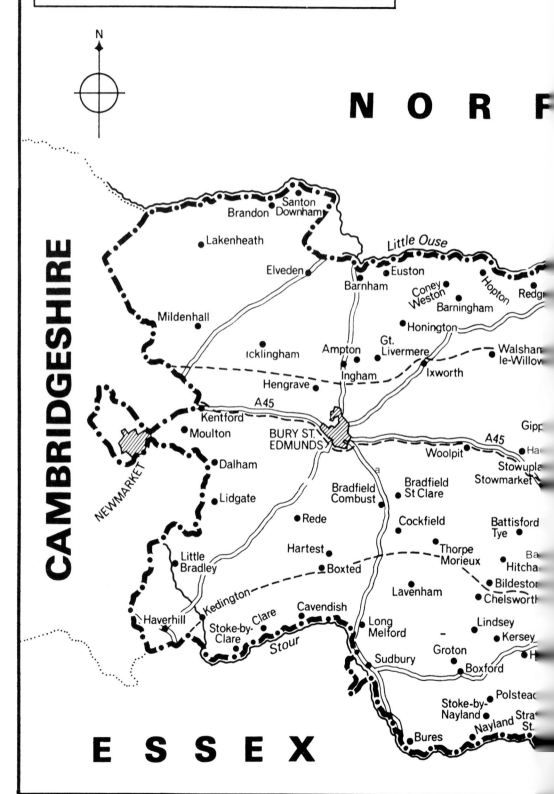

SUFFOLK

N

NORF

CAMBRIDGESHIRE

Santon
Brandon Downham
Lakenheath
Little Ouse
Elveden Euston Hopton
Barnham Coney Redg
Weston
Mildenhall Barningham
Honington
Icklingham Ampton Gt. Walsham
Livermere le-Willow
Hengrave Ingham Ixworth
A45
Kentford Gipp
Moulton BURY ST. A45
EDMUNDS Woolpit Ha
Dalham Stowupla
a Stowmarket
Bradfield Bradfield
Combust St Clare
Lidgate Rede Cockfield Battisford
NEWMARKET Tye
Hartest Thorpe Ba
Little Boxted Morieux Hitcha
Bradley Lavenham Bildesto
Kedington Chelsworth
Cavendish Lindsey
Haverhill Clare Long Kersey
Stoke-by- Melford Groton H
Clare Stour Boxford
Sudbury
Polstead
Stoke-by- Stra
Nayland Nayland St.
Bures

ESSEX

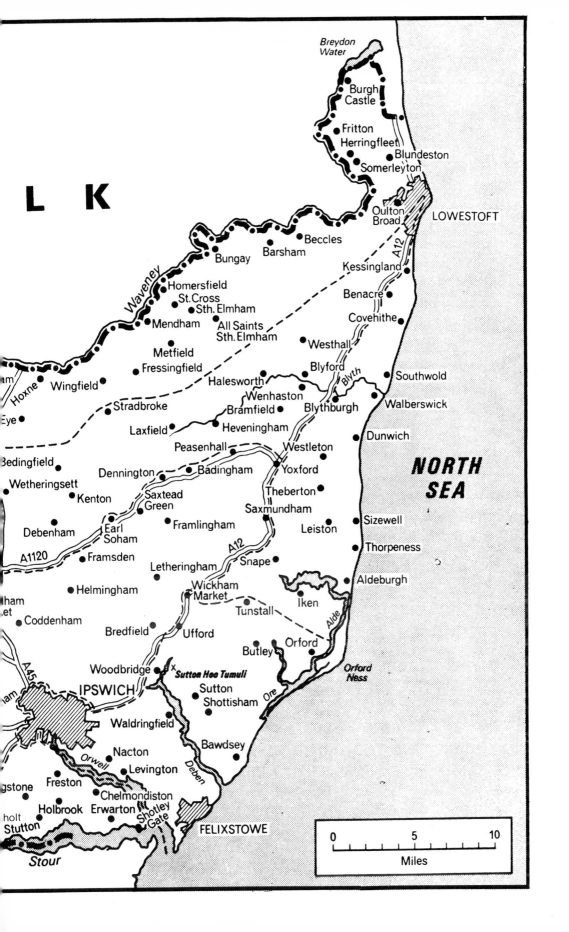

Stoke-by-Nayland church, its 120-ft brick tower soaring from a ridge above the River Stour. One of the favourite subjects of the painter, John Constable.

The gatehouse of Gedding Hall, one of the many moated manor and farm houses in Suffolk.

St Stephen's chapel near Bures. On this site King Edmund of the East Angles was crowned on Christmas Day 855. Consecrated in 1218 by Archbishop Stephen Langton, the chapel was used in later centuries as a barn. Restored, it now houses monuments to three earls of Oxford brought from Colne Priory in Essex.

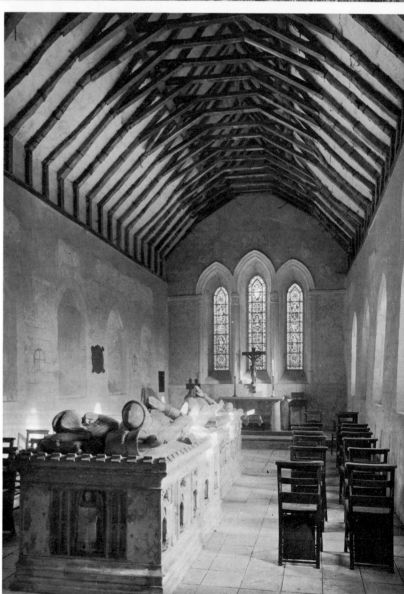

Hadleigh church, beneath which is thought to lie the tomb of Guthrum, the Christianised Dane to whom Alfred the Great conceded the monarchy of East Anglia. On the left is the 15th-century deanery tower.

A bench end in Hadleigh church depicts the severed head of St Edmund, killed by the Danes, in the jaws of a guardian wolf which restored it to his followers. There are many other symbolic associations with the East Anglian king and martyr throughout the county.

The 16th-century Weaver's House at Stratford St Mary. The wool trade brought prosperity to East Anglia and to Suffolk in particular from the fourteenth to sixteenth centuries.

Below This wooden cage serves as East Bergholt belfry, the church tower having never been completed. John Constable was born in the village in 1776, and his mother and father are buried in the churchyard.

Facing page Willy Lott's cottage near Flatford features in some of Constable's most famous paintings and in the East Bergholt memorial window to the artist. Willy himself lies in the churchyard.

Flatford Mill, now maintained by the National Trust, was one of a number of watermills and windmills owned by John Constable's father. 'The sound of water escaping from mill-dams, willows, slimy posts and brickwork – I love such things,' wrote the painter.

Wissington church, with a boarded
ll-cote more characteristic of neigh-
uring Essex than Suffolk. The interior
s a rare Norman chancel arch and
orways, and some 13th-century
ll-paintings.

e watersplash across Kersey's steep
ain street. In the great days of the
ol industry the village gave its name
a coarse cloth used mainly for men's
ear.

ght Little Wenham Hall, an early
ample of English brickwork.

n interior, Little Wenham Hall. The
uilding is preserved as an Ancient
onument.

Top left The double-humped bridge over the little River Brett at Chelsworth.

Above & left Polstead pond. The village is famous for its ancient Gospel Oak, and even more for the murder of Maria Marten, who is buried in the churchyard.

Right Maria Marten's cottage in Polstead. The Red Barn, scene of her killing, was destroyed by fire long ago.

Brent Eleigh Hall.

Brent Eleigh church. The monument to
'that good man, Edward Colman, the
last of an Ancient and Worthy family',
who built a parochial library on to the
church in the early 18th century.

Monks Eleigh: characteristic triangular village green, church, and parish pump.

Thatching a cottage in Monks Eleigh. Each thatcher has his own 'trade mark' pattern along the ridge.

Lavenham church, whose great landmark of a tower resulted from the thanksgiving of the 13th earl of Oxford for victory at Bosworth and the wealth of Thomas Spring 'The Rich Clothier'.

The front of Lavenham Guildhall. Here the prosperous clothiers met to argue about wages and prices and to settle their professional disputes.

Right A room on the first floor of the Guildhall. After the decline of the wool trade the building was used as a prison, kept in such bad condition that escaping felons could kick their way out through the plaster.

Left Long Melford: the green, church, and Elizabethan almshouses known as the Hospital of the Holy Trinity, refashioned in Victorian times.

The Adoration of the Magi, depicted on an alabaster plaque in the north aisle of the church. For some time this was hidden away, probably to escape the attentions of William Dowsing, the Cromwellian fanatic who devoted himself to the destruction of all holy pictures and carvings.

The Clopton chantry within the church. Substantial remains of verses can be seen painted along the wooden cornice, composed by John Lydgate, court poet to Henry VI.

Left Long Melford church. The walls display the finest examples of the county's speciality, 'flushwork' – a mingling of knapped flint and freestone in elaborately chequered patterns.

Melford Hall (South Front), where Sir
William Cordell entertained Queen
Elizabeth I at the beginning of her tour
of the county in 1578.

Left The great hall, *right* the staircase.

The 15th-century Priest's House at Clare. The decorative plasterwork is known as pargeting. Local craftsmen have left many examples of this, varying from simple representations of ropes and birds' feet to more inventive designs.

Left Clare Priory, the first English establishment of the Austin friars in the 13th century. After the Dissolution many of the buildings became out-houses, but much has now been returned to religious use.

Top right The abandoned station at Clare, on what was once the Stour Valley line. In the background is all that remains of the 13th-century castle keep.

Right Kentwell Hall, Long Melford. A Tudor house built for the Clopton family, who contributed so much to the church.

The statue of Suffolk's other great painter, Thomas Gainsborough, at Sudbury. His family home has been turned into a museum in the street named after him.

Thatched cottages at Cavendish, twice restored in recent years after damage by fire. Sir John Cavendish, who stabbed Wat Tyler at Smithfield in 1381, hid his valuables in the church belfry and fled from vengeful rebels, but was captured and killed.

ffords Hall, Wickhambrook. A 15th-
ntury house built on the site of an
rlier home of the Giffords.

detail of the solar, Giffords Hall.

Ickworth House. The elliptical rotunda was begun in 1794 by the fourth earl of Bristol to house his family and his collection of paintings, silver and furniture; but the entire building was not completed, by his son, until 1830.

Below The curving arm of the west wing seen from the rotunda. A similar wing balances it on the east, giving an overall length of about 600 feet.

Opposite the Pompeiian room. House and superb gardens are now administered by the National Trust.

Bury St Edmunds. The abbey gateway, torn down in 1327 by the townsmen in protest against monastic taxes and tyranny, but rebuilt after leaders of the revolt had been hanged or outlawed.

Facing page The abbey ruins, looking towards the high altar. Here Archbishop Stephen Langton and 25 barons met on St Edmund's Day in 1214 to swear that they would force King John to accept their Magna Carta of liberties and laws.

Infilling of the old abbey walls with later dwellings. Controversy still rages as to whether these anachronisms should be removed.

The Abbot's Bridge, crossing the River Lark near what was once the East Gate to the town.

A gilded oak cherub and the Royal Arms of Charles II in the Cathedral of St James the Greater, heart of a new diocese of St Edmundsbury and Ipswich created in 1913.

Opposite The bishop's throne. Extensions to the cathedral were completed by 1970 to mark the 1100th anniversary of St Edmund's martyrdom. Armoral shields of the Magna Carta barons were presented by an American society known as the Dames of Magna Carta.

roof of the new choir in the
hedral.

carved boss in the north porch of St
ary's church, named the Notyngham
rch after its donor, John Notyngham,
grocer of Bury.

upola House in the street called the
raverse. Over the door is a plaque to
e memory of Daniel Defoe, who said
f the town 'there is the appearance of
easure upon the very situation, and
iose that live at Bury are supposed to
e there for the sake of it'.

The Corn Exchange, bearing above the colonnaded portico the appropriate legend, 'The Earth is the Lord's and the fullness thereof'.

The Unitarian or Pentecostal Chapel in Churchgate Street, dating from the early 18th century.

The grandstand at Newmarket racecourse, around which the Suffolk and Cambridge County boundary does some bewildering contortions.

engrave church. The monument to
omas D'Arcy.

engrave Hall, a 16th-century building,
ow a convent school for girls. Once it
as the home of the Gage family,
hose 18th-century Sir William gave
is name to the greengage, which he
troduced to England from France. It is
aimed that the original tree still
ourishes in the grounds.

Culford Hall, built in the late 18th century for the Marquess of Cornwallis, associated with defeat at Yorktown but triumph in India. King Edward VII frequently came here for shooting parties. It is now a Methodist boarding school.

Below West Stow Hall, showing the timber and brick-nogging of the oversailing upper storey.

Right The red-brick gatehouse bears the arms of Mary Tudor, sister of Henry VIII. Her tomb is in St Mary's church, Bury St Edmunds.

Elveden Hall seen from Elveden church. The original Georgian building was adapted in the 19th century to suit the tastes of the Maharajah Duleep Singh, antiquary and sportsman who settled here.

Right Elveden Hall interior. The white marble hall, inspired by the Taj Mahal.

Euston Hall, home of the dukes of Grafton. The original buildings were badly damaged by fire in 1902 and reduced in size after the Second World War. The parkland was landscaped by William Kent in the 18th century.

Right Euston village.

Left Euston Hall seen from the south, across the lake.

Right A Breckland path near Cavenham.

A monument in Redgrave church to
Sir John Holt, the great lawyer and
Chief Justice.

Below The south porch of Woolpit
church. The name of the village does
not, as one might suppose, derive from
the prosperous wool trade, but from a
pit in which the last wolf in Suffolk was
killed.

Below right Bacton church roof, with
fading figures of a medieval Doom on
the wall.

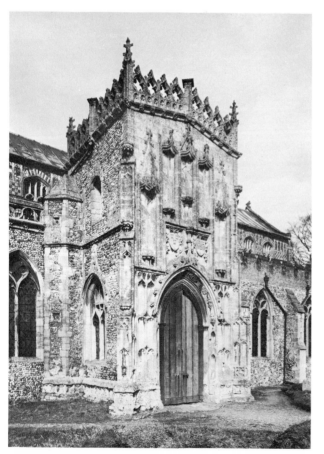

church and farmhouse at Earl Stonham. The church interior boasts hammer beams
rivalling those of the more celebrated Needham Market.

Below Coddenham, the Roman *Combretonium*. What was once an old inn has
become a private house and a post office, covered with 17th-century geometrical
pargeting.

Below right The watermill at Needham Market.

Haughley Park, a 17th-century manor house burnt out in 1961 but later restored.

Below The thatched church at Thornham Parve, within which is a rare 15th-century painted altarpiece rediscovered in this century.

Right Saxtead Green post mill. The buck, or body, is rotated to keep the sails facing into the wind. It is maintained in working order, open to the public, as an Ancient Monument.

Framlingham castle, given by Henry I to Roger Bigod but later demolished because of the rebelliousness of that Norman baronial family. Rebuilt at the end of the 12th century. Here Bloody Mary raised her standard in 1553 when there was a threat of Lady Jane Grey usurping the throne.

Below A biblical relief on the tomb of Fitzroy, Duke of Richmond, Henry VIII's illegitimate son. Here Adam and Eve are being driven from the Garden of Eden.

Right A representation of Noah's Ark on the Richmond tomb.

tomb in Framlingham church of
of the powerful Howard family,
held the castle in the 16th century.
helmet worn by the Earl of Surrey
n defeating the Scots at Flodden
gs above the tomb.

Moat Hall, Parham. A romantic moated grange, now a farmhouse. In a now-demolished hall nearby, George Crabbe came visiting Sarah Elmy until at last he could afford to marry her.

A bench end in Dennington church. This is the only known carving in England of a skiapod, a fabulous creature with one huge foot, under which it could shelter when the desert sun became too hot.

The north front of Heveningham Hall, built by a wealthy merchant family of Dutch descent, one of them M.P. for the nearby 'rotten borough' of Dunwich. Threatened with abandonment in the late 1960s, it was bought for the nation and put under the care of the National Trust.

Following pages
The interior of the building is largely the work of the young James Wyatt, who took over from the original architect, Sir Robert Taylor, when the exterior was almost completed. The entrance hall, with its fine vaulted ceiling and walls in green and white, is said to be the finest neo-classical room in Britain.
The Etruscan room at Heveningham is decorated according to a fashionable enthusiasm for the discoveries at Pompeii in the 18th century. The figures in the panels are painted in the terra-cotta shade of Etruscan vases. (Cf. the Pompeiian room at Ickworth.)

A statue of Justice above the covered market cross at Bungay. In olden times justice was administered below by exposing malefactors in a cage to the taunts of the public.

Top right Holy Trinity church, Bungay, built about the year 1000, with its round tower added in 1041.

Right Bungay castle – like Framlingham, a Bigod fortress which showed defiance rather than gratitude to the King. In the 18th century its then owner tried to sell off the stone for road-mending, but found the walls too sturdy to be demolished.

Barsham church, above the valley of the River Waveney. The round tower and thatched roof are familiar local features, but the trellis pattern of the east end is unique.

The south porch of Beccles church. Here Catherine Suckling came from Barsham to marry Edward Nelson and become, in due course, the mother of Horatio Nelson.

Far right The detached bell tower. For some time the fabric was unsafe for the ringing of its ten bells, but restoration began in 1974.

The 14th-century façade of Wingfield castle, complete with imposing gatehouse, is in fact little more than a façade; but the Tudor wing is finely preserved, and the castle is still in private occupation.

Somerleyton Hall, an Elizabethan house transformed by the flamboyant railway contractor, Sir Morton Peto, into what his neighbour and enemy, George Borrow, called 'a pandemonium in red brick'.

The entrance Hall, Somerleyton. The house and its attractive gardens are open to the public on certain days between Easter and September.

Oulton Broad, near Lowestoft, is linked by rivers and 'cuts' with the Norfolk Broads. It has a regatta in August, and frequent sailing and power-boat meetings.

Burgh Castle, the remains of the Roman *Gariannonum*, one of the forts built in third century A.D. to defend the coast against Saxon raiders.

ow left Fritton church: the Norman chancel.

mnants of Second World War defences on the crumbling cliffs at Covehithe, north Southwold.

Gun Hill, Southwold. The cannon are said to have been presented by the Duke of Cumberland in gratitude for the town's support against the Jacobites.

Facing page
Southwold lighthouse, built in 1899. The sign of the Sole Bay Inn, to the left, recalls the great battle fought between English and Dutch in 1672, when the Duke of York (later James II) and his cousin Prince Rupert established their headquarters in the town.

Southwold's inshore life-boat, a fast Atlantic 21, with the town spread out behind it. (courtesy of the RNLI, Southwold)

The market place and Swan Hotel, Southwold.

Detail of a screen in Southwold
church.

Church Lane, Blythburgh. The village
was a major port until the cutting of a
new channel between Southwold and
Walberswick altered the course of the
River Blyth.

Blythburgh church, used as a stable by
Cromwell's men and as an auxiliary
concert hall during the modern Aldeburgh Festival. The interior has some
grotesque bench ends portraying the
Seven Deadly Sins.

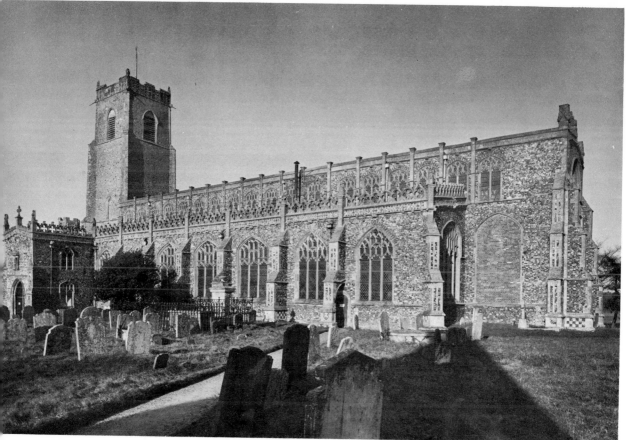

Looking from the Southwold bank of the River Blyth towards Walberswick.

Walberswick holiday houses, with Southwold in the distance across the River Blyth. The name of the village, wonderfully mispronounced locally, derives from the Saxon *wald*, a wood; *berige*, a hiding place; and *wye* or *wig* – a winding stream or, possibly, a heathen temple.

Ibberswick church was so neglected
after Henry VIII's appropriation of tithes
and other ecclesiastical assets that
much of the original fabric had to be
pulled down and the materials sold. At
the end of the 17th century a more
compact church was built around the
south aisle of the original.

A provider of galleys for the King's fleet,
and centre of many religious foun-
dations, Dunwich was once a major
east coast port. Persistently attacked by
the sea, it was almost completely
washed away by the 18th century,
though the tower of one of its churches
survived on these eroded cliffs until
1921.

Westleton village sign, recalling a windmill demolished only in recent times.

Below The duck-pond.

Facing page
Theberton church, in whose graveyard are buried the crew of a Zeppelin shot down in 1917.

The ruins of Leiston Abbey, a Premonstratensian foundation whose restored Lady Chapel now serves as a diocesan house of retreat.

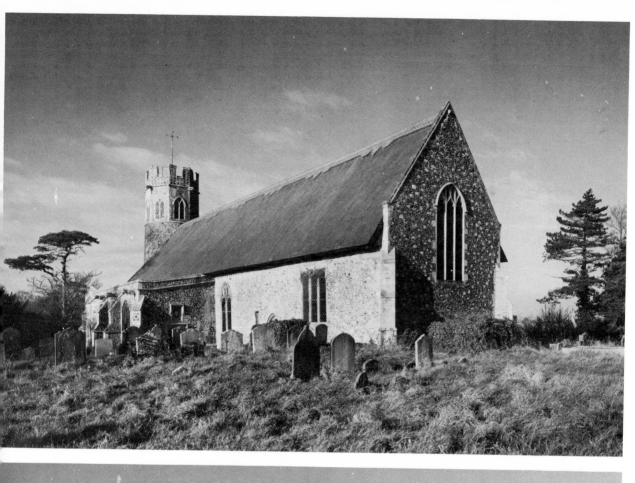

Thorpeness windmill and 'The House in the Clouds', a water tower incorporating living accommodation. The entire community is a 'Merrie Englande' fantasy contrived in the reign of George V.

Aldeburgh beach – the landscape of George Crabbe's *The Borough* and, consequently, of Benjamin Britten's opera *Peter Grimes*.

Aldeburgh life-boat: a 'beach boat' always in position, with many willing hands ready to shovel accumulated shingle off the ramp at an emergency launch.

Watching over Aldeburgh's model boat pond is this statue of a dog, erected by the people of the borough in memory of a much loved doctor and his pet.

The Moot Hall, Aldeburgh's Tudor council chamber, once with a market on the ground floor. An outer staircase to the first floor has led to the threat in all local legal proceedings: 'They'll have you up the steps.'

Facing page
The River Alde at the southern end of Aldeburgh, where the originally more important community of Slaughden existed until dragged into the sea.

Looking back along the shingle bank towards Aldeburgh from the top of its Martello tower.

Below A view across the marshes at Snape, continually threatened with inundation of salt water through the sea and river walls.

Beside Snape quay on the River Alde, work was begun in 1966 on the transformation of the old Maltings into a superb concert hall, to become the centre-piece of the annual Aldeburgh Festival. Opened in 1967, it was gutted by fire in 1969 but restored in time for the opening of the 1970 Festival.

Right The River Alde near Iken Cliff, where some of the earliest Iron Age immigrants settled, and where there were once busy quays for the schooners and barges of the coal and corn trade.

Looking from the sea wall towards Orford, a one-time borough which prospered from the wool trade and shipbuilding, but is now better known for smoked fish and for the avocets which nest nearby.

The keep of Orford castle, all that remains of a fortress built by Henry II to guard against invasion from the sea and against his own rebellious barons within.

Facing page
Quay Street, Orford. At the top is the church for which Benjamin Britten's well-known Canticles were originally conceived.

The quay, Orford, from which for many years workers took the daily ferry to the Secret Weapons Research Centre on the shingle spit where radar was first developed.

A Gothick folly gatehouse for the now-demolished Rendlesham Hall.

Top right Ivy Lodge, Rendlesham. Somewhere within these grounds Redwald, first Christian king of East Anglia, is thought to have held court.

The 14th-century gatehouse with its rows of carved heraldic shields is all that remains of Butley Priory, founded in 1171, when the River Butley came close enough for barges to deliver building stone for its construction.

Woodbridge tide mill, the last of its kind to be tidally operated: it worked until 1956. The wide expanse of the River Deben here is a flourishing centre of dinghy sailing and boat-building.

The Shire Hall, Woodbridge. Edward
Fitzgerald, translator of Omar Khayyam,
lived for many years above a gun-
smith's to the right of the building.

The Olde Bell and Steelyard, a Woodbridge inn which retains the device
once used for weighing wagons and
their loads of produce.

Three church fonts: *above* the Tournai font in St Peter's, Ipswich; *and* Boxford church.

Right An angel (the face probably disfigured by the Cromwellian iconoclast, William Dowsing) on the font at Sutton.

Docks and the Old Custom House on Common Quay, Ipswich. The early 13th-century
seal of the borough shows a sailing ship of the kind which, plying up and down the
River Orwell, made Gippeswic – later Ipswich – a flourishing port from earliest times.

Christchurch Mansion, an Elizabethan building presented to Ipswich by one of the
Cobbold family. Now a local museum with a picture gallery named after Cardinal
Wolsey, and some Gainsborough paintings of the River Orwell.

The Ancient House in Ipswich's Butter Market. Parts of a sequence symbolising the then known continents: at the time of this plasterwork, Australia had not yet been identified.

Right Elaborate pargeting on the façade of the Ancient House. The royal arms are those of Charles II. Originally Sparrowe's House, the building was occupied by successive generations of the same merchant family from Elizabethan times until the middle of the 19th century.

Two of Ipswich's twelve surviving
medieval churches:
Left St Margaret's, on the edge of
Christchurch Park.
Right St Lawrence's. The tower, with
its varied flushwork, was much rebuilt
in the 19th century.

The gateway of Wolsey's College, all
that remains of the great Cardinal's
dream of a mighty scholastic foundation in his home town of Ipswich.
The arms above the door are those of
Henry VIII, who used Wolsey and then
discarded him.

corner post of a house in Found-
n Street, Ipswich.

e Jacobean gateway to Erwarton
l.

llowing pages
eston Tower, a Tudor folly built by an
swich merchant near Pin Mill, on the
ver Orwell.